Mythic Heroes

Angela Royston

Ginn

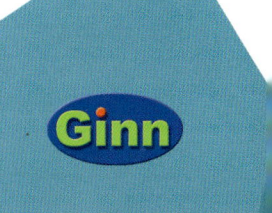

Heroes and Myths

Who are your heroes? Are they footballers, movie stars or superheroes like Spiderman? People long ago had heroes too. They heard about their heroes through poets and singers (the pop stars of the past!) who told stories about them. The stories were passed from person to person and as they were told and retold, they became more exciting and fantastical. They became **myths**.

As you hear each hero's story, write down and keep your answers to each **QUIZ** question. (Remember, the answers are in the book!) Let the stories begin!

In this book you can enter the mythic worlds of Hercules, Odysseus, Beowulf and King Arthur. Their stories are so amazing that we even know about them today – **hundreds** and **thousands** of years later!

Heroes Hall of Fame

I used my strength to complete not one, but 12 difficult tasks!

PAGES 6 TO 11

Hercules: The Strong Man

Odysseus: The Great Adventurer

It took me 10 years to get home from battle!

PAGES 12 TO 17

Penelope:
The Loyal One

I set a clever test to outwit my husband's rivals!

PAGES 18 TO 19

Monsters and dragons were no match for me!

PAGES 20 TO 25

Beowulf:
The Brave Warrior

King Arthur:
The Legendary King

I won many battles with the help of Excalibur and the knights of the Round Table.

PAGES 26 TO 31

Hercules: The Strong Man

Scroll-File

NAME:
Hercules
(pronounced Her-cue-lees)

HEROIC QUALITIES:
Physically strong and brave

FAMOUS FEAT:
Achieved the impossible, not once but 12 times!

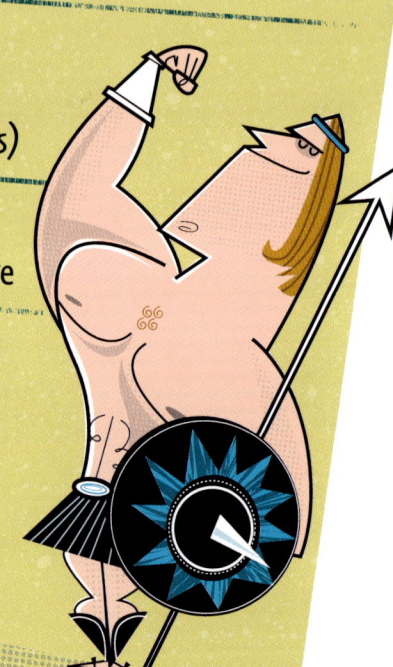

Hercules was a hero from ancient Greece.

The goddess Hera always hated Hercules, even from the moment he was born! She sent snakes to kill him when he was a baby, but Hercules killed them with his bare hands!

Then, when Hercules grew up, Hera put a spell on him that made him murder his wife and family. When Hercules realised what he had done, he felt terrible and went to the god Apollo for help.

Apollo told him that if he could complete 12 very difficult tasks he would not feel guilty any more.

Hercules's first task was to kill a fierce lion that lived in the hills of Nemea. Ordinary weapons couldn't kill this lion! Instead, Hercules blocked one of two entrances to the lion's cave and then trapped the lion in the other entrance. Hercules attacked the lion with his bare hands and choked it to death!

After killing the monstrous lion, Hercules took the lion's skin and wore it as a cloak!

Hydra was a poisonous snake with nine heads. She was really confident that Hercules couldn't kill her! Why? Well, if one of her heads was cut off, another grew in its place! But Hercules did manage to kill her … As he cut off her heads, one by one, his nephew sealed her necks with fire so they couldn't grow back! Finally, Hercules cut off her last head and buried it under a rock!

Hercules's last task was the most difficult one of all. People in ancient times thought that when they died they passed into the Underworld – the world of the dead. The entrance to the Underworld was guarded by a monstrous creature called Cerberus. Cerberus had **three heads** – each one a fierce, snarling dog's head with snapping, sharp teeth. And, as if that wasn't enough, Cerberus's back was covered with snakes' heads! The task? Hercules had to capture Cerberus and bring him back alive!

Hmmm... Tricky!

FuLL-SCHeDuLe FaCT

Hercules was a busy man with 12 tricky tasks to complete! These tasks included capturing a crazy boar, a rampaging bull and a herd of man-eating horses, as well as stealing golden apples from a dangerous dragon! Exhausting!

QUIZ The snake that Hercules killed had **** heads.

Odysseus: The Great Adventurer

Scroll-File

NAME:
Odysseus
(pronounced Oh-dee-see-us)

HEROIC QUALITIES:
Cunning and clever and a brave fighter

FAMOUS FEAT:
Planning the Trojan horse

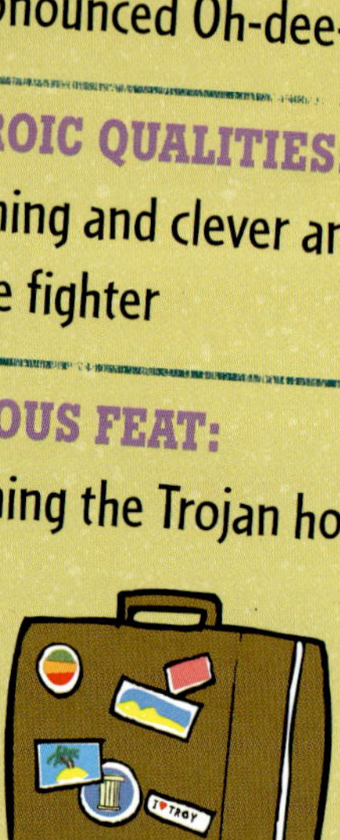

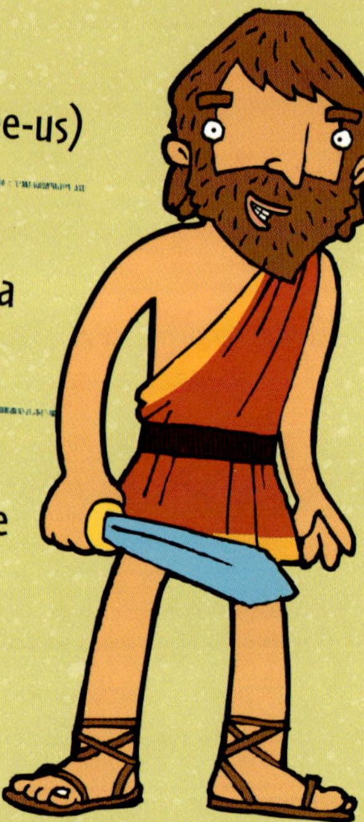

Odysseus was the heroic King of Ithaca in ancient Greece. He fought in battle for the Greeks and helped them to capture the city of Troy. After the battle, Odysseus and his men set sail for home. Little did Odysseus know that his journey home would last **10 YEARS!** He would face many adventures on the way and would need all his cunning to get home safely …

FooLeD-You FaCT

Odysseus had a cunning plan to get the Greek army into the city of Troy! The Greeks gave the Trojans a huge wooden horse as a peace offering. The Trojans pulled the horse inside the city walls. That night the horse's belly opened – Greek soldiers jumped out and captured Troy!

On Odysseus's journey home, his troubles began when he stopped to rest on an island. Unluckily for him, it was the home of the Cyclops. One of the Cyclops captured Odysseus and his men, and trapped them in a cave. How would Odysseus get out of this one? Well, Odysseus got the monster drunk on wine and then used a burning stake to blind the Cyclops's huge eye. Odysseus and his men then hot-footed it back to their ship.

Phew!

Cyclops wanted revenge! So he asked his father (the sea god, Poseidon) to make Odysseus's journey home hard and long!

Odysseus's Dilemmas

I am Poseidon, the god of the sea. I whipped up a storm and wrecked Odysseus's ships. (That'll teach him to mess with my son, the Cyclops!)

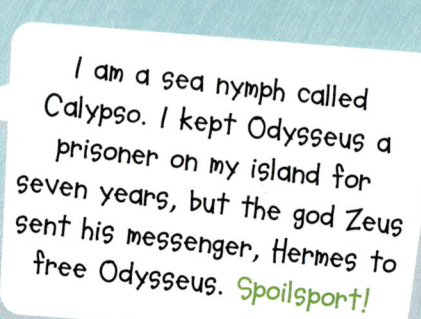

I am a sea nymph called Calypso. I kept Odysseus a prisoner on my island for seven years, but the god Zeus sent his messenger, Hermes to free Odysseus. Spoilsport!

16 QUIZ The Trojan horse was a scheme dreamed up

Penelope: The Loyal One

1

Penelope was Odysseus's wife. While Odysseus was battling to get home, everyone told Penelope that her husband would never return. Many men were eager to marry Penelope, but she still loved Odysseus and did not want any of them.

2

So Penelope set these hopeful men quite a task. She said she would marry the first man to string Odysseus's great bow and shoot an arrow. (She hoped they'd all fail!)

Beowulf: The Brave Warrior

Scroll-File

NAME:
Beowulf
(pronounced Bay-ah-wolf)

HEROIC QUALITIES:
Brave and strong, loyal and generous

FAMOUS FEAT:
Killing the monster called Grendel

Beowulf was a warrior for the Geats, who lived long ago in southern Sweden.

Across the water from the Geats lived the Danes. The Danish king had built a magnificent hall where his people could feast and have fun, but their fun was about to end!

A monster called Grendel was so jealous of the hall that he left his home in the swamp and murdered everyone who dared to stay in the hall!

Beowulf heard about the **terrifying murders** and set sail with his men to help the Danes kill Grendel.

One night, Beowulf and his men waited in the hall for Grendel to come. Beowulf bravely decided to fight Grendel without weapons, armour or a shield. (What a show off!) Soon enough, Grendel crept into the hall …

FaMiLY FaCT

Grendel's mother wanted revenge for her son's death, so she attacked the Danish hall. Beowulf headed into the swamp to kill Grendel's mother, but she quickly dragged him down to her lair. Luckily, Beowulf found a magic sword and used it to kill Grendel's mother. Two down …

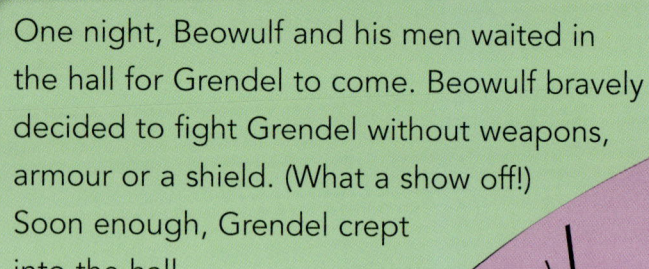

Beowulf kept Grendel's arm and proudly hung it on the wall of the hall to show that he was the winner. Yuk!

Grendel killed one of Beowulf's men, so Beowulf grabbed hold of Grendel and held on so tight that the monster couldn't escape. They wrestled until Beowulf ripped off Grendel's arm at the shoulder. Injured, Grendel crawled back to his lair in the swamp, where he later died from his wound.

Beowulf returned to the land of the Geats and eventually became king. He ruled for 50 years before disaster struck ... A thief awoke a dragon that was coiled around a hoard of treasure in its underground den (Not such a clever thing to do!). The dragon was so angry that it rampaged around the countryside, burning down people's homes with its fiery breath. Although he was old, Beowulf knew he had to fight the dragon ...

QUIZ To help the ✶✶✶✶✶, Beowulf killed a monster

Beowulf's armour couldn't protect him from the dragon's **scorching flames** and his sword slid off the dragon's scales. The dragon sank its fangs into Beowulf's neck! **Ouch!** Luckily one of Beowulf's men came to the rescue and stabbed the dragon in the belly – and this weakened the dragon's flames. Beowulf then gathered his strength and killed the dragon with his dagger. But Beowulf was so badly burnt that he died soon after he slayed the dragon.

King Arthur: The Legendary King

Scroll-File

NAME:
King Arthur

HEROIC QUALITIES:
Brave fighter and excellent horseman

WEAPON:
Excalibur

COMPANIONS:
Knights of the Round Table and Merlin the wizard

Arthur was a heroic king from medieval Britain.

He was adopted as a baby and no one but Merlin the wizard knew that the king was his father.

When the king died, he left no heir. Instead, it was said that whoever could remove a magic sword from a block of stone would become the new king. So the challenge was set!

Knights of the kingdom came from far and wide, but no one succeeded in pulling the sword from the stone.

Finally, Arthur decided to have a go and to everyone's amazement he slid the sword easily from the stone! The peasant boy became king!

When Arthur became the king, he and his knights fought many battles against neighbouring kings who wanted to conquer his lands. With his trusty **magic sword**, Excalibur, by his side, King Arthur was invincible! All the knights felt honoured to fight for Arthur, but they quarrelled amongst themselves. Why? Because they wanted to know who was Arthur's favourite knight! But Arthur had no favourite – he made the knights sit at the Round Table, so they were all equal!

All the knights at the Round Table were heroes, known for their strength and courage, but Sir Galahad would become an even bigger hero.

There was one empty place at the Round Table and only a knight who was pure and virtuous could sit there. One day, a name appeared on the empty seat. Whose name was it? It was Sir Galahad's. When Sir Galahad joined the other knights and took his seat at the Round Table, a vision of the Holy Grail appeared.

Turn over to find out more about the Holy Grail ...

A name is appearing!

I hope it isn't Sir Brian!

...or Sir Wilfred. Have you seen the state of his armour?

It was said that The Holy Grail was a cup that had once held Christ's blood.

It could give food to the knights and heal the sick. So the knights of the Round Table decided to go in search of it!

King Arthur was too old to go with them and he sadly said farewell to the knights as they went their separate ways to look for the Holy Grail. He knew many of them would never return.

30 QUIZ King ★★★★★★ made his knights sit at th

FRIENDSHIP FACT

The Lady of the Lake gave Arthur the sword, Excalibur, but made him swear to return it before he died. So, true to his word, before he died, Arthur sent a knight to throw the sword back into the lake. The Lady of the Lake thrust her hand out of the water to catch the sword!

So who was the first to find it? Well, Sir Lancelot came close, but he couldn't see it because he wasn't pure enough.

The knight who found the Holy Grail was … the pure and virtuous Sir Galahad, of course! The Grail was so holy that only the purest knights could see it.

"I can't see it!"

"Where is it?"

Juggle with the first letters NODGAR and you get the name of the fiery creature that one of our heroes killed – DRAGON!